All About
Martin Luther King, Jr.

Todd Outcalt

BLUE RIVER PRESS

Indianapolis, Indiana

All About Martin Luther King, Jr.
Copyright © 2016 by Todd Outcalt

Published by Blue River Press
Indianapolis, Indiana
www.brpressbooks.com

Distributed by Cardinal Publishers Group
Tom Doherty Company, Inc.
www.cardinalpub.com

ISBN: 978-1-68157-091-4

Author: Todd Outcalt
Series Editor: Charleen Davis
Editor: Dani McCormick
Interior Illustrator: Amber Calderon
Book Design: Dave Reed
Cover Artist: Jennifer Mujezinovic
Cover Design: David Miles

Printed in the United States of America

Contents

To the Ten Point Coalition

All About
Martin Luther King, Jr.

Preface

Dr. Martin Luther King, Jr. was one of the most influential Americans of the 20th century. He is remembered for his leadership in the civil rights struggles during the 1950s and 1960s in the American South. Dr. King is also remembered for his powerful speeches and sermons, his philosophy of "nonviolent resistance," and his commitment to ending segregation, unjust laws, and poverty.

Martin Luther King, Jr. was not always famous. In fact, he grew up like other African American children in the South and experienced many forms of racism and segregation. Segregation was a part of Martin's childhood and this system—which treated black people and white people differently—impacted him in many ways.

Long before Martin began speaking about civil rights and leading marches, he had experienced racism in his own life. His father, also named

Martin, was a Baptist pastor, and he taught young Martin that segregation was wrong. These many conversations and experiences with his father would shape young Martin's life in powerful ways and would, in fact, prepare him to be a great American leader.

Although Martin's life ended violently, he will always be remembered for his peaceful marches and for his speeches about social change. He will be remembered for making a difference for millions of Americans. Every year, on the third Monday of January, Americans celebrate Martin Luther King, Jr. Day as a national holiday. This holiday is near Martin's birthday (January 15) and is a day when all Americans can look back and remember Dr. King's legacy. It also allows Americans to remember that the dream of equality and the promise of justice for all is still a work-in-progress.

When we remember Martin Luther King, Jr. we are not only remembering a great American, but a great person. Dr. King said that he wanted to be remembered as a person who "gave his life in the service of others." He wanted to be re-membered as a person who fed the hungry and loved other people—regardless of race.

The National Civil Rights Museum was built around the Lorraine Motel where Martin was assassinated

Today, many streets across America are named after Martin Luther King, Jr. Buildings and memorials across the nation preserve his memory too, including the National Civil Rights Museum in Memphis, Tennessee. But Martin's influence was much greater than brick and stone. He is remembered for his actions and his words.

Dr. Martin Luther King, Jr. was a great American, but his story had humble beginnings.

Martin Luther King, Jr. speaking at a rally in 1966

Chapter 1
Growing Up

Martin was born on January 15, 1929 in Atlanta, Georgia. He was a beautiful baby and when he was born his parents were very happy. Martin was their second child and they felt very blessed to have him in their family.

Martin's birth-home in Atlanta, Georgia

What many people do not know, however, is that when Martin was born, his parents named him Michael after his father. However, when Martin was five years old, his father decided to have both of their names changed. Both Michael Sr. and Michael Jr. became Martin Luther—a name that had spiritual significance.

The inspiration for the name change came from Martin Luther, a church reformer who had lived in Germany in the 1500's. *That* Martin Luther had set out to reform the church in his day and was an inspirational leader to Martin King, Sr., who was a Baptist pastor. Martin Sr. had read many of Luther's writings and felt inspired by his teachings about faith and life. He felt inspired by Luther's leadership during a time of crisis.

Now Martin had a new name—and as we shall see—a new identity, too.

Young Martin grew up in a loving home with his father, Martin Sr. and his mother, Alberta Williams King. He had an older sister, Willie Christine, and a younger brother, Alfred Daniel.

The three children got along well and loved each other. They were a happy family. Since his father was a Baptist pastor, many of Martin's early experiences centered around church and home.

Alberta Williams King, Martin Luther King, Sr.,
Jennie Celeste Williams (Alberta's mother),
Alfred Daniel King, Willie Christine King, and
Martin Luther King, Jr. pose for a family photo

In the black community in Atlanta, Martin Sr. was well-known. He often took young Martin Jr. to the church office when he went to work or with him to visit people's homes. Martin grew to love the church. He sang in the church choir at his father's parish—the Ebenezer Baptist Church in Atlanta—and attended youth meetings there.

Martin would preach in front of the choir
at his father's church, Ebenezer Baptist Church
in Atlanta, Georgia

Martin's mother, Alberta, was a soft-spoken woman who was very dynamic and respected within the community. She had a college education—which was an achievement few African American women of the time could imagine. Nevertheless, Martin's mother was a humble and gracious woman who helped her husband, Martin Sr., in his pastoral work. She also tried to shelter Martin as much as possible from the realities of segregation.

As Martin Luther King, Jr. grew, he began to have other experiences that would shape his life and his thoughts about race and segregation. For example, when Martin was very young, his best friend was white and lived across the street. When the boys became old enough to go to school, the white boy's parents would no longer allow him to play with Martin.

Martin's friend went to a white school. Martin had to go to a school for black students. Schools were just one way that segregation was experienced. There were many other forms of segregation too.

Businesses and stores were also segregated. Different drinking fountains for black people and white people existed. These were often marked as "Black" and "White." Restrooms were also marked in this way. Many times blacks weren't allowed to use public restrooms at all. Often, instead of "Black" the sign read, "Colored."

Drinking fountains on display at Birmingham Civil Rights Institute show how much segregation affected everyday life

African Americans had to sit in the balcony at the movie theatre as well. Public buses were another place where segregation was clearly visible. Black people were forced to sit in the back of the bus while white people got to ride up front.

Young Martin experienced these and other forms of racism and segregation as he was growing up. There were times when racism showed up in the form of name-calling or discrimination. Often African Americans were not allowed to live where they wanted to live or work where they wanted to work because of their race.

Many busses like this one were segregated, forcing African Americans to sit in the back where it was hotter and less comfortable

Most of these laws in the South were called "Jim Crow Laws" and were "rules" that were generally accepted and strictly enforced.

Like his father, young Martin wanted to see changes in the South, but these changes became all the more real to him after he graduated from high school. Martin was a good student and, like his parents, wanted to have a college education. Martin's college days would shape his life and his mind in many ways. His family and his education would prepare him to be a great American leader.

Young Martin Jr. dressed for school outside his
childhood home in Atlanta, Georgia

Chapter 2
College Bound

During the years when Martin was attending Booker T. Washington High School in Atlanta (a school named after another famous black American) he continued to experience many forms of racism. But Martin did not let this discrimination hold him back. He was able to skip his freshman and senior years of high school

Booker T. Washington High School, built in 1920, was the first all-African American public high school in Georgia.

because he was a top student. At the age of fifteen he entered Morehouse College in Atlanta where he earned a degree in sociology.

Martin graduated Morehouse College in 1948.
His sister would graduate from the all-girl
Spelman College the same year

After graduating from college in 1948, Martin decided that he wanted to be a Baptist pastor like his father. During his high school and college years, Martin often preached in churches, and people were impressed by his powerful sermons and his insights. His father was proud of him,

Martin Luther King, Jr. preaching at
his father's church after graduation

too and encouraged him to stay at Ebenezer to serve the church. Martin did want to serve the church. He had been ordained in 1947 while he was still in college, but he wanted to have different experiences too. He wanted to be a pastor, but he wanted to learn as much as he could. He also told his father that he wanted to attend a school in the North.

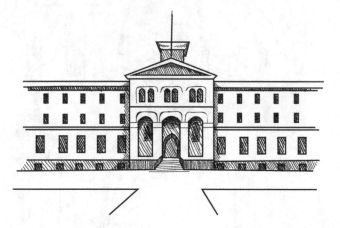

Crozer Theological Seminary taught many aspiring black and white students to be Baptist leaders

Martin enrolled at the Crozer Theological Seminary located in Chester, Pennsylvania—a school that was very different from the all-African American Morehouse College in Atlanta. Here, in this northern graduate school, Martin was among white students. He was one of only six African American students.

Right away it was apparent to the professors that Martin was going to be the top student in his class and he was. He was also adopting many of the teachings of Jesus to address the racial problems and tensions in the South. Martin believed that Jesus was right about "loving your enemy", "loving your neighbor as yourself" and "turning the other cheek." He believed that these Christian principles could help to bring about change in people's hearts if they were applied to the Civil Rights struggles of the South.

Martin also discovered other influences. He read books and essays written by Henry David Thoreau—an American abolitionist and a philosopher. Thoreau had written one essay entitled, "On Civil Disobedience" in which he said that it was the duty of people to refuse to cooperate with evil systems and laws. Thoreau was thrown into jail because of his peaceful protests against unjust laws. Martin took these thoughts and practices to heart and began adopting them into his philosophy.

Martin reading in the library of the
Crozer Theological Institute in 1956

During his seminary days, Martin Luther King, Jr. also studied about Mohandas Gandhi—a man who had led the nation of India in its independence from the British Empire. Gandhi, though a Hindu, was influenced by the teachings of Jesus to create a nonviolent approach—helping the people of India to overcome their own forms of racism and segregation.

Gandhi's nonviolent resistance showed Martin it was possible to cause change without harming anyone

Little by little, Martin Luther King, Jr. was forming an approach that would help him lead people through their own struggles. He knew that he would return to the South, but he had one more step to take.

Because Martin was such a good student, he decided that he wanted to earn a Ph.D. He was accepted as a student at Boston University.

Boston was very different from Atlanta in the 1950s; black people and white people lived and worked together more freely.

While he was a student at Boston University, Martin's life also changed in other ways. There, he met a beautiful young lady named Coretta Scott. She was from Alabama and was studying to be a singer. When Martin and Coretta went on their first date they talked about their own families and the struggles back home.

Martin knew right away that he wanted to marry Coretta, as they shared a Southern background and many of the same ideas about America. On June 18, 1953, Martin and Coretta were married in Marion, Alabama. Then they went back to Boston to live while Martin finished his Ph.D.

When Martin graduated from Boston University, he became *Dr.* Martin Luther King, Jr. He had a great deal of education and had many ideas about how he could help people. Now it was time to begin his work.

Martin Jr. and Coretta are married by Martin Sr. in 1953 at Coretta's parents' house

Soon after graduating, he received many job offers from churches. Martin could have had jobs in New York, Massachusetts, and in other northern cities. He seemed to be in great demand.

In the end, Martin decided to move to Montgomery, Alabama and become the pastor of the Dexter Avenue Baptist Church. Moving to Montgomery was a decision that would change both Martin's and Coretta's lives. The decision would eventually change the lives of millions of other Americans too.

The Dexter Avenue Baptist Church was built
in 1883 and was the second all-African American
church in Montgomery, Alabama

Chapter 3
Martin Becomes a Leader

When they moved to Alabama, Martin and Coretta knew that their lives would not be easy in the South. Still, it was their home and they wanted to raise their own family in the South, no matter how difficult it would be.

America was changing in many ways. Martin and Coretta were interested when they heard that a case involving an African American girl named Linda Brown had made it all the way to the Supreme Court. Linda Brown wanted to attend a white school in Topeka, Kansas, but the principal of the school refused to admit her. On May 17, 1954, all of the judges agreed that "separate" schools for blacks and whites could not be "equal." After this ruling, all schools across the country had to accept both black and white students without discrimination.

Unfortunately many schools in the South refused to abide by this court decision. The *Brown v Board of Education* ruling was the beginning of a movement. Martin understood that if people came together, America could change.

Linda Brown stands in front of the school
she wanted to attend in 1954

During his first year as the pastor at Dexter Avenue, Martin was very busy. He encouraged people to become involved in the National Association for the Advancement of Colored People (NAACP) and to vote. This organization had been established in 1909, and was an organization devoted to helping minorities find jobs, apply to schools, and register to vote. Dr. King understood that all of these were important,

The NAACP worked with churches to encourage voting in the black community

but he knew that voting could change laws. New laws would eventually change how people lived.

Martin and Coretta had a baby girl, Yolanda Denise, on November 17, 1955. Martin was proud of his little girl and he wanted the best for her. He wanted to be a good father and a good pastor. Shortly after Yolanda was born, Martin heard about the bravery of a lady who also lived in Montgomery. Her name was Rosa Parks.

Martin and Coretta play with their first child
in Montgomery, Alabama in 1956.

One day, Rosa Parks was on a bus that got crowded. The driver told her that she had to move farther back in the bus as the white section of the bus was full. He needed another row for white riders and Rosa was sitting in the first row of the black section. It was a law that African Americans had to sit in the back of the bus, but Rosa was tired and refused to give up her seat. When Rosa Parks refused to move to the back of the bus, she was arrested.

Rosa Parks was forty-two years old when she was arrested. This event helped advance a

Rosa Parks helps arrange a bus boycott with Martin Luther King, Jr. in 1955.

growing Movement for civil rights and equality. Martin brought city leaders and others from the black community together to talk about how they could help Rosa. They also formed a plan that was called the "bus boycott." Rosa Parks was inspired by Martin, and she said later of him, "It seemed as if every time he spoke, he said something I wanted or needed to hear."

The bus boycott was the first organized form of protest of unequal civil rights. Martin became the leader of the bus boycott. He urged all African Americans all over the city to refuse to ride the bus until the laws were changed. Many people had to walk for miles to get to work. Others rode in the cars of their friends or neighbors. The city buses were quickly losing money because most of the people who rode the buses were black.

There were white leaders in the Montgomery city government who were angry. They saw black people organizing for change, but there were also white people who were part of the Movement too. This angered the Montgomery leaders, especially the police and business owners. They

saw African American people walking, riding bi-
cycles, and carpooling all over town.

Martin stands next to a bus near the end of
the Montgomery bus boycott in 1956

Although this was a peaceful protest, many
African American people—including Martin—began receiving threats. Eventually Martin was arrested and soon after someone threw a firebomb
onto the porch at his house. It was a frighten-
ing time for Martin, Rosa Parks, and the black
community of Montgomery. They did not ride
the buses for over a year until, eventually, the

U.S. Supreme Court ruled that the Montgomery buses had to allow equal seating for whites and blacks.

Many people walked instead of driving during the Montgomery bus boycotts in 1956.

On December 21, 1956, Martin and other leaders began riding on the buses again. They sat wherever they liked. It was a great, joyous day! The Civil Rights Movement was just beginning, and many people were now looking to Dr. King to lead the way

A few months after the success of the Montgomery bus boycott, Martin and other

African American leaders met in Atlanta. They wanted to start a new organization that could help African American people all over the South. They called it the Southern Christian Leadership Conference (SCLC). Martin was elected president of the organization.

Martin had an opportunity to help others in a new way. He wanted others to implement the nonviolent movements and ideas that he had learned from Jesus, and Thoreau, and Gandhi. Now he was not just leading people in Montgomery, but all over the South.

People listened to what Martin had to say. They agreed to follow a nonviolent path as they protested unjust laws. Under Martin's leadership there was a new spirit afoot, and the people knew change was possible after the success of the Montgomery bus boycott.

In May of 1957, thousands of people gathered on the steps of the Lincoln Memorial in Washington, D.C. This was called the Prayer Pilgrimage and took place on the third anniversary of *Brown vs. The Board of Education,* celebrating the brave young black girl who wanted to be the best student she could be. Martin was one of many speakers that day. Everyone who walked was urging Congress to pass a Civil Rights bill that would guarantee equal rights under the law.

Martin arranged and walked in marches to urge Congress to pass a Civil Rights bill

They hoped that the President, Dwight D. Eisenhower, would lead the nation in making these changes, but this continued to be a struggle. There were more marches and other boycotts. And there would be many bad times before things improved in the South.

Martin's "I Have a Dream" speech, given in front of
the Lincoln Memorial, is still quoted often

Chapter 4
Marching Toward Freedom

In 1960, there were many changes in the nation and in Martin's household. Martin and Coretta had a growing family, with a second child born the previous fall. His name was Martin Luther King, III.

The Kings celebrate the birth of their first son,
Martin Luther King, III

Although Martin's family was safe and happy, it was apparent that other struggles were emerging. People in America did not agree about many things and there was a growing tension.

There was a new nonviolent protest in 1960 that many young people participated in across the South. Most lunch counters would admit only white people. African Americans who supported change began sitting at these "whites only" lunch counters and there were many arrests. The most famous of these sit-ins was in

Four students from the North Carolina Agricultural and Technical College stage a sit-in at the famous lunch counter in Greensboro, North Carolina in 1960

Greensboro, North Carolina. It drew the most attention to the growing Civil Rights Movement.

Richard Nixon and John F. Kennedy had the first televised presidential debate in 1960

In 1960, two presidential candidates, John F. Kennedy and Richard M. Nixon, debated each other on TV. This was the first time in history that people had been able to see presidential candidates on television.

During the months when Nixon and Kennedy were running against each other, Martin had other changes in his life. He had moved his family from Montgomery, Alabama to Atlanta, Georgia. He had to say goodbye to the people of Dexter Avenue Baptist Church, but was now the leader of a nationwide movement.

Martin was arrested thirty times
between 1956 and 1967

Shortly after moving to Atlanta, Martin was arrested in Atlanta, Georgia at a lunch counter sit-in and he was put in jail. Martin's wife, Coretta, was worried. It appeared that there was no way for Martin to be released, but Coretta received a call from John F. Kennedy saying he would help. John F. Kennedy's brother, Robert, began working with the officials, paying Martin's bail, so that he could go home.

The election year of 1960 was very important for the Presidency. There was a growing concern about the racial tensions in America. Poverty was a big issue, and there were also worries about the possibility of a war in Vietnam.

John F. Kennedy eventually won the election. He was a supporter of Dr. King and the struggle for Civil Rights. John F. Kennedy was also the first Catholic to be elected President.

Then in 1961, there was a new surge in the Civil Rights Movement as many people from the North began taking buses to the South to help with the cause. These people—both black and white—were called Freedom Riders. The Freedom Riders would stage sit-ins not only at "whites-only" lunch counters, but also in bathrooms, stores, and train stations. They would sit-in to protest the separate areas for blacks and whites.

Freedom Riders rode from Birmingham, Alabama
to Montgomery in 1961 and were attacked
by an angry mob

Many communities in the South did not want
Freedom Riders in their town, so the Freedom
Riders were often threatened. Sometimes the
bus tires were slashed. Sometimes people were
shot at. There were verbal taunts and sometimes
rocks were thrown at the Freedom Riders.

Dr. King and the Civil Rights leaders had prepared everyone, however, for these nonviolent
protests. They would not fight back or resist

arrest. Many would go to jail, be released, and then return to carry on the protests in another town.

During this time, when Martin was speaking often to groups and urging them to stay strong, the people would sing a song. "We Shall Overcome" became the song of the Civil Rights Movement and everyone believed the words from the song, "Deep in my heart, I do believe, that we shall overcome some day."

The struggle for freedom and changes in the laws did not come quickly. Some cities refused to change. As more and more people supported the Civil Rights Movement, and travelled south to help, tension grew. Sometimes these tensions led to change. But other times they led to violence.

Chapter 5
To Birmingham

In 1963, many important events impacted the Civil Rights Movement and the nation. The Civil Rights Movement continued in communities across the South. Sometimes the peaceful demonstrations brought change, but many times there was resistance. Sometimes laws were changed. And at other times judges and city leaders refused to budge.

But the Movement was growing and Martin and the leaders of the Southern Christian Leadership Conference were eager to push forward with a new plan. After one meeting in April of 1963, a decision was made to organize a new march in the city of Birmingham, Alabama.

This was a bold decision, as Birmingham was one of the most segregated cities in the South. Although nearly half of the population of the city was African American, laws still kept most of the black community from voting. The schools remained segregated despite the Supreme Court ruling. Only a handful of very powerful white men controlled the city, including the police force.

Birmingham also had a well-known police commissioner named Theophilius Eugene "Bull" Connor. Everyone in the city was afraid of Bull Connor. He made life especially tough on the African Americans citizens, and many were arrested simply for speaking out for Civil Rights.

Protestors of all ages joined together

As the Movement came to Birmingham, there was also a new strategy. The organizers openly asked black people to stage sit-ins at lunch counters, to speak in churches about nonviolent protest, to sing freedom songs like "We Shall Overcome", and to march in the streets for freedom. The black community was also asked to boycott white businesses.

Protesters like Walter Gadsden, a 17 year old, were attacked by police dogs

All of these forms of protest made many white people in Birmingham angry. Bull Connor attempted to disperse the marchers by using clubs. He also released vicious police dogs on the crowds. But the marchers stayed strong and peaceful.

During the Birmingham March there were numerous reporters and photographers who recorded the events as they unfolded. Stories were written in the newspapers, and many people, even in other cities across the South, were astounded by the brutality of the police.

But the protests in Birmingham continued, and after ten days over five hundred people had been thrown into jail. Few had money to post bail. Many families were worried. But the Movement was growing stronger, not weaker.

Then, on April 12, Martin and the other leaders were preparing to march again through the streets of Birmingham. Martin's wife, Coretta, was close to the delivery date of their fourth child back in Atlanta. She was worried about Martin being in Birmingham and wished that he were home.

Martin and the other leaders knew that if they marched, he would probably be arrested. And this is exactly what happened. Martin had been in jail before, but the jail in Birmingham was harsher. He was not allowed to speak to anyone

Martin was arrested in Birmingham on April 12th, 1963 and placed in solitary confinement where he wrote "Letter from Birmingham Jail"

or to make a phone call to Coretta. In fact, he was placed in a dark cell by himself and for many days was all alone. While Martin was in jail, his wife, Coretta gave birth to Bernie Albertine King.

Eventually some friends brought Martin a newspaper article that had been written by eight prominent pastors in Birmingham—all white pastors—which expressed their opposition to Martin Luther King, Jr. and the protests. These white pastors believed that Martin was an "outsider" who had come to Birmingham to agitate and cause trouble. They believed that protests did not belong in the streets, but that change should come through the courts only. They also said that what Dr. King and marchers were doing was against the law.

Martin used any paper he could find to write his letter, including scraps of paper from a ceiling tile manufacturer

Dr. King knew that he had to respond to these charges from the other pastors. He wrote a letter in the margins of a newspaper, on scraps of paper, and a legal pad that his lawyer gave him.

When he was finished, his letter was published in several newspapers around the country and in the *Christian Century*, a magazine in Chicago.

This letter became known as "Letter from Birmingham Jail" and is one of the most famous letters ever written. The letter also addressed many of the concerns that white people had, and Dr. King gave a reasoned response to all of them.

First, Martin pointed out in his letter that "injustice anywhere is a threat to justice everywhere." He pointed out that all Americans had a right to speak and live and travel anywhere in America that they liked. Martin wrote that the Civil Rights Movement was based on love and not hate and used faith to address other fears. He wrote that Jesus and other past heroes had also been regarded as trouble-makers in their day.

When Martin was released from jail after eight days, he did not leave Birmingham. Instead, he and the leaders formed yet another plan. They would invite children to march for freedom. Some thought this was dangerous, but others believed that Bull Connor and the police would not harm children.

Firefighters used high-powered fire hoses on young protesters in Birmingham in 1963

On May 2, 1963, thousands of children and teenagers marched through the streets of Birmingham. True to his word, Bull Connor attempted to break up the protest. The police used clubs again, and they released attack dogs. In addition, they used powerful water hoses to disperse the crowds.

There were thousands of people around the country who were watching this march on TV. When people saw the brutality against children and teenagers, they were angry! People demanded change in Birmingham.

In the next few days, business leaders in the city met with the organizers. They agreed African Americans needed better treatment in Birmingham. They approved of allowing white and black alike to eat at lunch counters. Unfortunately, it took much longer for most of these promises, and others, to be fulfilled.

Nonetheless, Martin and the leaders did sense that they had won a great victory in Birmingham. People in cities across the South knew that change was possible. They believed that if change could come to Birmingham, then it could be achieved anywhere. Laws began to change in many cities in the South and businesses, schools, and parks were slowly becoming integrated.

Martin and the leaders were now seeing great changes in America, but they needed to do more. They would soon turn their attentions to the nation's capital. Washington, D.C. was the next stop.

Chapter 6

On to Washington, D.C.

In June of 1963, President John F. Kennedy began working with Congress to pass a Civil Rights Bill. The President, as well as many in Congress, believed that the laws had to change. They believed that all Americans should have equal access to public buildings, businesses, and schools. They believed that restaurants, hotels, movie theatres, and stores should become racially integrated.

The Civil Rights Bill was a large step forward, and Martin and the other Civil Rights leaders felt that their presence in Washington, D.C., the nation's capital, would be important to passing this legislation. A march was soon organized and on August 28, 1963, there were nearly 300,000 Americans who gathered for the rally.

People came from across the country to march. They were from the North and the South. They were rich and poor. Many had travelled great distances and made many sacrifices to be there. Other Americans watched on TV.

Eventually people made their way to the steps of the Lincoln Memorial. There were many who spoke that day about the need for integration. They spoke about changing laws and becoming a better nation, but people remember Martin's speech the best.

Dr. King had come to Washington, D.C. with a prepared speech, but as he had done on many occasions before in churches and at marches, Dr. King felt moved to speak from his heart. He began his prepared speech, but then Mahalia Jackson, a gospel singer who was standing next to Martin on the podium, asked Martin to "tell them about the dream." Martin then began preaching, and he ended with words he had preached in Detroit some weeks before.

That day, Martin said many things that Americans remember, but mostly they remember Martin saying, "I have a dream." It was a powerful moment. Dr. King used many words from the Bible too. He quoted from the prophet

Isaiah when he said, "The rough places will be made plain, and the crooked places will be made straight. And the glory of the Lord shall be revealed, and all flesh shall see it together." He also used familiar phrases that all Americans knew like when he said that America should "let freedom ring."

Millions of Americans saw Martin's "I Have a Dream" speech in front of the Lincoln Memorial in 1963

Dr. King closed his speech with the words, "Free at last. Free at last. Thank God Almighty, we are free at last."

A member of Congress, who heard Dr. King speak that day, said that Dr. King, "Educated, inspired [and] informed ... not just the people there, but people throughout America and un-born generations." The March on Washington had a powerful effect upon America and is one of the most important moments in our nation's history. Dr. King's speech was also the first time that many Americans had heard him speak.

Unfortunately there were still many people who were opposed to integration or changing the laws. Though 1963 was a year of great pro-gress, it was also one of great sadness.

On September 15th, 1963 the 16th Street Baptist Church in Birmingham, Alabama was bombed as the congregation was gathering for worship to hear a sermon entitled, "The Love that Forgives." Twenty-two people were injured, and four young girls were killed. Fourteen year-old girls, Addie Mae Collins, Cynthia Wesley, and Carole Robertson, and eleven year-old Denise McNair all died in the blast.

People across the nation were shocked and horrified by this hatred. More people began call-ing for change. Martin asked President Kennedy

IN MEMORY OF

DENISE MCNAIR **CYNTHIA WESLEY** **ADDIE MAE COLLINS** **CAROL ROBERTSON**

THEIR LIVES WERE TAKEN BY UNKNOWN PARTIES ON SEPTEMBER 15, 1963 WHEN THE SIXTEENTH STREET BAPTIST CHURCH WAS BOMBED.

"MAY MEN LEARN TO REPLACE BITTERNESS AND VIOLENCE WITH LOVE AND UNDERSTANDING"

Many newspapers across the country printed reports about the church bombing, sparking outrage

for help, and the President sent several FBI agents to help Martin keep the peace in Birmingham. It was a dangerous time and many people were fearful and angry.

Just a few weeks after this bombing, on November 22, 1963, President Kennedy was shot and killed in Dallas, Texas as he was riding in a convertible through the streets of the city. Lee Harvey Oswald was arrested, and then killed by Jack Ruby before his trial could begin. The nation seemed to be unraveling and tensions were high. There was also a deep sadness as the nation mourned Kennedy's death.

President John F. Kennedy's assassination came at a time of high tension throughout the country.

For Martin and the other leaders of the Civil Rights Movement, the work would go on. They wanted to remember the four girls who had died and President Kennedy. They believed the best way to honor them would be to see that the Civil Rights Bill was signed into law so that all Americans could be free at last.

The year 1963 had been a remarkable one of highs and lows. It was a year of triumph and tragedy. They hoped 1964 would be better.

Chapter 7
A Year to Remember

After President Kennedy was killed, Lyndon B. Johnson, the vice-president, became our nation's leader. There were many issues that the new President had to address, including honoring President Kennedy's memory.

President Johnson was working with Congress on a Civil Rights Act. The President invited several nationally-known Civil Rights leaders to the White House. Among these were Roy Wilkins of the National Association for the Advancement of Colored People (NAACP), James Farmer of the Congress of Racial Equality (CORE), Whitney Young with the Urban League, and Dr. Martin Luther King, Jr., who was still heading the Southern Christian Leadership Conference. The President wanted to hear what these leaders had to say, but he also wanted their input on what the Civil Rights Act should include.

In particular, Martin was helpful in assuring the President that his organization and the others, would support the outcomes of the Act and work for the continued advancement of African Americans with these new laws. President Johnson also believed that Martin's voice, in particular, would help bring attention to the need for a Civil Rights Act and would help him to work effectively with Congress to pass it.

President Johnson signed the Civil Rights act surrounded by his advisors and prominent supporters of the Act, like Martin

On July 2, 1964, President Johnson signed the Civil Rights Bill into law. This was one of the most important pieces of legislation in our nation's history and is still important today. Essentially, the Civil Rights Act of 1964 meant that segregated schools could no longer exist; segregated schools had to integrate or face legal consequences. Also businesses, hotels, restaurants, and other public places could not discriminate. States that practiced discrimination in their laws would not receive federal money. The Civil Rights Act ensured, too, that all Americans could register to vote and could not be denied a vote.

When President Johnson signed this bill into law, Dr. Martin Luther King, Jr. was standing next to the President. This was a great honor for Martin, a greater day for the nation.

Still, just because a bill had been signed into law did not mean that people would be willing to change. There was still discrimination and segregation. Martin and the other leaders continued to press for change. It seemed slow in coming, and many people were becoming impatient and angry.

At 35 years-old, Martin was the youngest person
to ever receive the Nobel Peace Prize

Most of all, Martin hoped that America
would find a peaceful solution to these problems. Others agreed with him. In December of
1964, Martin was awarded the Nobel Peace
Prize. This prize, established in 1895 by Alfred
Nobel, is a great honor. It is given every year to
"the person who shall have done the most or the
best work for fraternity between nations, for the

abolition or reduction of standing armies, and for ... promotion of peace."

Martin flew to Norway to receive this honor and he also gave an acceptance speech. In this speech, given on December 10, 1964, Martin stressed the importance of seeking peace through love. He said he believed that African American people would one day "overcome."

Martin spoke to the realities of the time in America. He pointed out that, just the day before his acceptance speech for the Nobel Peace Prize, that more than forty churches had been bombed or set on fire in Mississippi alone. Many people were still suffering.

The prize was accepted by Martin on behalf of the whole Civil Rights Movement and he used the prize money of $54,000 to help bring peace to America. While this was a great day for Martin, he knew that segregation and poverty were still the greatest enemies that America was facing. He wanted to do more. He wanted to see true equality in America.

As soon as Martin returned to the United States, he noticed new challenges. Many people were still not registered to vote and he believed that this step was vital if people were to participate in changing the laws. Martin and the leaders went to places like Selma, Alabama. There they set up voter registration drives. They also marched to the courthouse to register people for the vote.

As a result, many people were arrested, including Martin. Once again, Martin wrote a letter from jail. His letter was published and Americans read that there were nearly as many black people in jail in Selma as were registered to vote. It was a troubling time.

There were also new ideas afoot in America in 1965. Some people in the African American community were growing weary of waiting for change. They did not like the idea of nonviolent marches, registration drives, and being arrested for breaking the Jim Crow laws. Some younger black leaders, such as Malcolm X, believed that

Although Malcolm X and Martin did not have the
same methods, they both fought for civil rights

the black community had to fight back with
their fists.

Martin and others in the Movement still believed that nonviolent resistance worked best.
This belief was consistent with Martin's faith,
and he had seen how nonviolent protests had
brought change to India years before. Martin
had received the Nobel Peace Prize and he
wanted peace to come through love and through
practicing the teachings of Jesus and methods of
Gandhi.

The Selma Marches were having an impact on the nation. More people were registering to vote, and there was much discussion. Eventually the nation's eyes would be tuned in again to Selma and the marches there. And Martin would be leading the way yet another time.

Martin and Coretta appeared in the *New York World-Telegram and Sun* in 1964

Chapter 8
The March from Selma to Montgomery

In 1965 it seemed that every march was more important than the previous one. This was especially true in Alabama.

George Wallace, the governor of Alabama, did not like the nation's attention being focused on his state. He did not want the marches being held in Selma or in other cities across Alabama. At the time, Alabama still had a very hard literacy test that voters needed to pass before they could vote. The test was deliberately difficult to keep black people, who had been sent to inferior schools for generations, from voting. This was just one of the laws that Martin wanted to see changed.

Tensions escalated as more people joined the marches in Selma. During a march on March 7, protesters were attacked by state troopers with tear gas and night sticks. Some troopers, riding horses, also trampled marchers. Once again, the Selma marches were on TV, and people across the country were outraged at the violence. This day became known as Bloody Sunday.

Martin lead the march from Selma to Montgomery in March 1965 surrounded by fellow protesters

On March 9, 1965, Martin and the other leaders organized a march that was to travel from Selma to Montgomery. They believed that a march originating in Selma and progressing to the state capital would bring attention to voting rights in the state of Alabama. In Selma, only 2% of the eligible black voters were registered, and there was great resistance from the local authorities to increase black voter registration. Thousands of people from all over the nation—both black and white—traveled to Selma to participate in the march. Many people who participated in the march are still alive today. It had become a symbol for the Civil Rights Movement and people were expecting change.

Martin asked everyone in the march to remain peaceful and calm if they encountered resistance and threats. That day, as the marchers moved out of Selma toward Montgomery, they had to cross a bridge. Unfortunately when the people reached this point they were facing a wall of state troopers. Martin was leading the way, and people were holding hands and singing and marching in a peaceful manner.

Martin quickly realized that people would be hurt or killed if they attempted to cross the bridge. He asked the people to turn back, and promised to try again. These constant threats of violence, and the distance, made the protest a difficult and long one for the protesters.

After Governor Wallace refused, President Johnson sent troops to help protect the people on the third march attempt. On March 21, the march from Selma to Montgomery was underway again. By this time the numbers had grown even more. There were not only black people, but many white people who wanted to participate. The marchers came from many backgrounds and faiths, and everyone was holding hands and singing songs as they walked toward Montgomery. This was a beautiful day, and many people remember it. The March from Selma to Montgomery was about 54 miles and lasted five days.

Almost 25,000 marchers traveled together and handed a petition to Governor George Wallace. They demanded that all people in Alabama be allowed to vote. They wanted an end to the voting tests because they discriminated against the poorest citizens. The marchers knew that the poor needed to vote as much as anyone else in America.

August 8, 1965, President Johnson signed the Voting Rights Act into law that said no voting tests could be administered. The bill also allowed the federal government to appoint observers to oversee state and local elections. This would ensure that all laws were administered in the same manner throughout the country. In this way the march from Selma to Montgomery was a success.

Los Angeles Times

Looting and Fires Ravage L.A.
25 Dead, 572 Injured; 1,000 Blazes Reported

South L.A. Burns and Grieves

Newspapers across the country reported on the Watts Riots as people mourned the dead and injured

Just days after President Johnson signed the new voting bill into law, a young African

American man, Marquette Fry, was arrested by police officers in California. A crowd gathered to protest this arrest, tempers flared, and soon there was rioting and violence in the streets of Los Angeles, in an area called Watts. The rioting lasted six days and has come to be known as the "Watts Riots." Stores were burned and looted. There were taunts and insults. People were throwing stones.

Martin and the other leaders realized that discrimination was not the only problem that African Americans were facing. Poverty was a big problem too. When people became poor, they felt helpless and believed that they had no voice or influence. Martin and the other leaders believed that poverty was leading the nation toward class warfare. Some people were living in poverty while others were enjoying all of the freedoms of America.

Now the Civil Rights Movement turned its attention toward this poverty problem. This was the next step for Martin. He brought people together to discuss the stresses of poverty and they formed a new plan for addressing this problem across the nation.

On June 21, 1964, Dr. King addressed one of the largest crowds he'd ever spoken in front of. There were more than 70,000 people in attendance at the hopeful rally in Chicago.

Dr. King spoke again in Chicago on July 10, 1966 as part of Freedom Sunday. The SCLC joined with other groups who were also looking to make a change in the city and organized a rally. Martin spoke to the crowd and led a march

The King family: Dexter, Yolanda, Martin Luther Jr., Bernice, Coretta, and Martin Luther III

to Chicago City Hall, where he placed a list of demands on the door.

For nearly three years Dr. King and other Civil Rights leaders focused on the city of Chicago. This became known as the Chicago Freedom Movement and focused on issues of affordable housing, education, employment, and crime.

These challenges would also involve change, and Martin knew he would have to change too. He would have to lead the country in a new way from a new place, so in 1966, Martin moved his family from Atlanta, Georgia to Chicago, Illinois.

Although Chicago was not in the South, there was still discrimination and poverty in the northern city. Chicago had more than one million African American residents in 1966.

There were whole neighborhoods that were inhabited by the unemployed, the poor, and the needy. Most of the children had no place to play, so they played in the street. In some neighborhoods, on hot days children played around open fire hydrants.

Like many other cities across the country, Chicago seemed like a hopeless cause. There were not enough jobs and people had fallen into despair. They needed someone or something to give them hope. Martin wanted to lead another great charge for change in America, and now he would be doing it in Chicago.

The Chicago Skyline hid the poverty that Martin hoped to fix by organizing nonviolent protests and working with lawmakers

Chapter 9
Martin's Final Days

The summer that Martin moved to Chicago, he led several marches. Most of these peaceful protests were meant to address the conditions of poverty—a growing problem across the country. Many people, however, did not want to talk about poverty.

Chicago's Mayor Richard J. Daley showed no intentions to give in to demands to improve conditions for the poor

At that time, Richard J. Daley was the mayor of Chicago, and Martin wanted to have a meeting with him to talk about many of these problems. Martin hoped that the Chicago government would do more to provide jobs, build more low-income housing, and do more to stop police violence against African Americans.

Mayor Daley responded to Martin's requests, saying that these problems would be addressed, but nothing changed in Chicago. The problems continued. Eventually, though, changes were made that did impact the lives of the black residents of Chicago, including the Fair Housing Act, which was passed in 1968.

Throughout 1966 and 1967, there were other concerns that were occupying the attention of Americans. Since the late 1950's, America had become increasingly involved in a war in Vietnam. By 1966 there were many young Americans who were fighting a ground war in that country.

Americans were divided about this war. Every night, Americans saw images of the Vietnamese civilians burned by napalm bombs or the rising numbers of dead American soldiers. As the American involvement in Vietnam grew in 1967 and 1968, Americans paid less attention to the Civil Rights Movement.

Some African Americans began to call Martin an "Uncle Tom," or a traitor. Many young whites began to speak of "white power" while young blacks were calling for "black power." Other groups, such as the Black Panthers, no longer believed in Martin's vision of peaceful marches with black and white people working together for change.

There were many changes happening in America and in the Civil Rights Movement. Increasingly Martin turned his attention to addressing the issues of poverty as a means of bringing people together. This was in spite of many, including a large number of African Americans, who no longer saw a connection between poverty and the Civil Rights struggle.

Eventually Martin and the other leaders believed that people should march again to Washington, D.C. in the spring of 1968. This time, instead of Civil Rights, everyone would march for a "war on poverty." Dr. King and others hoped that this march would bring the nation together in new ways and help to heal the racial tensions of the country.

Martin joined the garbage workers of Memphis, adding his voice to their strike in hopes of addressing the problem of poverty.

When garbage workers in Memphis, Tennessee went on strike in the spring of 1968, Martin and some other leaders saw this as an opportunity to address the problem of poverty. And so Dr. King went to Memphis to march with the workers for better pay and better working conditions.

Many times during the Civil Rights Movement, Martin and the other leaders met with resistance from local authorities. But sometimes the resistance came from the federal government. As Dr. King was organizing his march in Memphis in 1968, he was served a restraining order by U.S. Marshall, Cato Ellis, forbidding a march in the city. Like many of these orders, Martin and the other leaders ignored this one and regarded it as unjust. They continued to organize marches around their philosophy of peaceful resistance.

But the first march in Memphis did not go as Dr. King had hoped. Instead of a peaceful march, some of the marchers in the group began breaking into local stores and looting. One of the peaceful marchers, Bernard Lee, said, "People in the march were breaking store windows. It had become violent internally and [we decided] that Martin Luther King needed to leave the march."

Dr. King did leave that day, but he came back to Memphis in April. He wanted to stand with the garbage workers, but he also wanted to organize a new march—one that would show the world that nonviolent marches were still possible, even in Memphis.

Yet, Dr. King was troubled. Since 1966 there had been an increasing number of threats on his life. At one march in Chicago he had been hit in the head with a rock. Although his head was bloodied and he had to be supported to stand up, he finished the march that day. However, in the spring of 1968, he could sense that some of the death threats were very serious.

On April 3, while addressing the new march in Memphis, Dr. King made a statement about his life near the end of his speech. He said, "I've been to the mountaintop ... and I've seen the Promised Land. I may not get there with you. But I want you to know that we, as a people, will get to the Promised Land."

The next day, Dr. King met with his friends in his second floor room at the Lorraine Motel in Memphis. Dr. King was troubled by the growing belief that violence was the best means of solving America's problems. Dr. King talked about the violence in Vietnam and why he was opposed to that war. He spoke about the soul of America and why he still believed that the teachings of his faith and the nonviolent resistance of Gandhi were the only ways to heal the country. He also told his friends that he did not fear death.

Hosea Williams, Jesse Jackson, Martin, and Ralph David Abernathy met in Martin's room at the Lorraine Motel the day before he was shot

Later that afternoon, Dr. King stepped onto the balcony outside of his hotel room for some fresh air. He was talking to some friends who were urging him to wear a coat. Suddenly there was the sound of a rifle shot and Martin fell onto the balcony. People began to scramble to help him. Others were pointing toward the roof where the rifle shot had come from.

In less than an hour the announcement was made that Martin Luther King, Jr. had died. Many people around the country mourned his death and promised to continue the causes that he stood for. The day was April 4, 1968. He was only thirty-nine years-old.

The word of Dr. King's death also brought a new wave of violence across the nation. There were riots in many cities. It seemed that America had lost its most powerful voice for peace. People wrote to Coretta Scott King, offering words of comfort and support. Jacqueline Kennedy, the widow of President John F. Kennedy who had been shot and killed some years before, wrote a letter.

As police searched for Dr. King's killer, they eventually arrested a man named James Earl Ray. His fingerprints had been found on the gun that was used to shoot Martin, and while in jail, he confessed to killing Dr. King. About a year after Dr. King's murder, James Earl Ray was sentenced to ninety-nine years in prison.

Five days after Dr. King had died, many people gathered for his funeral. This was a Tuesday, April 9, in Atlanta at the Ebenezer Baptist Church where Martin had first served as a pastor with his father. It was like going home again. The church was filled to capacity. There was music, and several people spoke about Dr. King. They

Martin's casket was walked through the streets of Atlanta in an old horse wagon

also played a recording of Martin's own words. Some of these words were from Martin's last sermon just a few days before.

Here is how he said he wanted to be remembered: "I'd like someone to mention that Martin Luther King, Jr. tried to give his life serving others. I'd like for somebody... to say that Martin Luther King, Jr. tried to love somebody. I want you to be able to say that day that I did try to feed the hungry... I want you to say that I tried to love and serve humanity."

After the funeral, the casket that contained Martin's body was placed on an old farm wagon. Dr. King had planned to use the wagon during the march on poverty in Washington, but now it was used to carry his body to its final resting place. The wagon was wheeled through the streets of Atlanta to Morehouse College for a public ceremony, about four miles away.

Coretta Scott King and the family led the huge funeral procession. Some estimate that nearly 100,000 people followed along behind the family and the funeral wagon. At Morehouse,

Benjamin Mays delivered a eulogy and Mahalia Jackson sang, "Precious Lord, Take My Hand."

Jesse Jackson, fellow civil rights leader, reads a newspaper reporting King's assassination

Later, at the cemetery, other people spoke, and then Martin Luther King, Jr. was buried beneath a large headstone. The words on the stone were appropriate to summarize his life and his legacy. They were words from an old African American spiritual that Dr. King had used in his "I Have a Dream" speech in Washington.

Martin and Coretta are buried at the Martin Luther King, Jr. National Historical site in Atlanta, Georgia

Free at last, free at last.

Thank God Almighty, I'm free at last.

Chapter 10
The Power of Dr. King's Words

As the Civil Rights Movement grew, so did Dr. King's influence and the power of his words. Not only was Martin often leading marches and demonstrations across the South, he was also traveling in order to give speeches, conduct interviews with reporters, and appear on television. People came to see Dr. King as the face of the Civil Rights Movement, but his words were often more powerful than his presence.

Martin and Coretta lead a march against poverty in Mississippi in 1966, at the March Against Fear

Martin was able to explain the American vision well and gave voice to the words of the United States Constitution and the laws of the land. People from all walks of life were swept up by his insights and his words. Martin was a powerful speaker and everyone—even those who disagreed with him—wanted to hear what he had to say.

As Martin's influence grew, people began to record his speeches. Television was a relatively new technology and was having a great impact on society. Instead of looking at photographs and reading day-old newsprint, people across the country, and the world, could now see what was happening as it occurred through television. Martin's appearances on television news, his interviews, and his many speeches were now being heard by millions, not just by those who were involved directly in the marches and the struggles for equality.

Other people also recorded Martin's speeches on vinyl records—and some of these records became quite popular. Martin's printed speeches and his essays were popular as well. His words, both recorded and in print, were becoming part of everyday conversations and discussions.

Because of Dr. King's education and his personal experiences, he was able to speak to people from all walks of life. He spoke not only to the powerful politicians and leaders in Washington, D.C., but also related to those who had no voice, to those who felt powerless due to their poverty, their race, or their lack of education. His words transcended race and class, and his appearances and speeches in the north often drew large audiences.

Martin met Robert Kennedy, President John F. Kennedy's younger brother, moments before he spoke about the need for civil rights in June 1963

By the mid-1960's, Dr. King was hailed not only as a Civil Rights leader, but as an orator of great power and persuasion. People would travel great distances to hear him speak. He began to receive awards and recognition for his writing and oratory skills.

In 1966, for example, Martin was elected to the fellowship of the American Academy of Arts and Sciences. His inclusion was a prestigious recognition of his writings that had helped to shape the Civil Rights conversations and those debates surrounding the American involvement in the Vietnam War. After Martin's death, his family was honored by Dr. King receiving a Grammy Award for "Best Spoken Word Album" for "Why I Oppose the War in Vietnam."

Many of Dr. King's words have become a part of history. He spoke about the realities of racism, poverty, and education. He frequently shared stories that could move people to action. His words have, in many ways, become timeless.

For example, Martin believed that injustice anywhere was a threat to justice everywhere. He also believed that many of society's ills were due to selfishness, and a lack of love and concern for other people.

Martin believed that holding on to hate was a far greater burden than one could bear. He believed that love—a deep concern for others—was true freedom.

He often spoke out about the injustices of his critics, who opposed equality for all Americans, but he also criticized supporters who remained silent out of fear. Martin believed that all Americans—not just the black community—needed to speak up and get involved in the Civil Rights Movement. Martin wanted all Americans to be committed to seeking justice and equality for everyone. He hoped that average Americans, not just political leaders, would make their voices heard and commit themselves to change.

When Martin and his friends were arrested or thrown into jail by the local authorities, his words would become even more powerful. Not only did Dr. King write "Letter from Birmingham Jail", but he frequently wrote essays and gave interviews during these difficult times. He never gave up hope.

Martin was arrested many times during his fight for justice and civil rights, but didn't see it as a setback

Dr. King said, "the ultimate measure of a man is not where he stands in moments of comfort and convenience, but where he stands at times of challenge and controversy." Martin never shied away from speaking of his own struggles, and challenged others to examine their own motives and desires.

Martin did not want people to stop pushing or shy away from the ongoing struggles for Civil

Rights. He wanted people to always maintain hope that change could be accomplished. He believed America would eventually live up to her reputation of freedom and equality. Dr. King wanted change to be accomplished peacefully not violently, because he believed violence only caused more problems. He once said, "Violence, as a way of achieving racial justice, is both impractical and immoral. I am not unmindful of the fact that violence often brings about momentary results. Nations have frequently won their independence in battle. But, in spite of temporary victories, violence never brings permanent peace."

There are now many monuments and memorials across the country and the world that have been built or dedicated to Dr. King's words. Many of these monuments preserve his ideas, not just his memory.

For example, the Lincoln Memorial in Washington, D.C. is etched with the beginning of Dr. King's "I Have a Dream" speech. Dr. King's words can be found on other monuments around the world. From Stone Mountain in Georgia to

Liberty Bell Park in Jerusalem, Israel, Dr. King's words are memorialized all over the world.

A plaque marks exactly where Martin stood while delivering his historic "I Have a Dream" speech in front of the Lincoln Memorial

Today, people can read Dr. King's books themselves. Among Dr. King's titles are: *Stride Toward Freedom: The Montgomery Story*, *The Measure of a Man*, and *Strength to Love*. His book *Why We Can't Wait*, published in 1964, is a detailed account of the nonviolent movement in the

South, but also contains some of his most memorable quotes. His book *Conscience for Change* was his final book before his death.

Many people have also written books about Dr. Martin Luther King, Jr. They don't regard him as just a historic figure or a great American, but as a global inspiration for peace. In the end, Martin is not a man who has passed from memory, but stays alive in the hopes and dreams of many Americans. His legacy is not only found in the streets, monuments, and buildings named after him, but in the thoughts and ideas that his words convey. People from all walks of life have found and continue to find inspiration and meaning in them.

Martin and Rosa Parks are remembered in many different ways, including street names in many cities all over the country

Martin wrote many books, but *Why We Can't Wait*
was his most popular and is still read
and taught all over the world

Select Quotes from Martin Luther King, Jr.

"It seemed as if every time he spoke, he said something I wanted or needed to hear."

— Rosa Parks was inspired by Martin, and she said this later about him.

"Injustice anywhere is a threat to justice everywhere."

— A line from "Letter from Birmingham Jail" that Martin composed to answer charges from clergy and to clarify issues for blacks and whites.

"The rough places will be made plain, and the crooked places will be made straight. And the glory of the Lord shall be revealed, and all flesh shall see it together."

— Martin quoted in his "I Have a Dream" speech the prophet Isaiah from Isaiah 40:4-5.

"Free at last. Free at last. Thank God Almighty, we are free at last."

— Famous closing lines to Martin's "I Have a Dream Speech."

"I've been to the mountaintop...and I've seen the Promised Land. I may not get there with you. But I want you to know that we, as a people, will get to the Promised Land."

— April 3rd, lines from a speech Martin gave in Memphis about his life.

"Violence, as a way of achieving racial justice, is both impractical and immoral. I am not unmindful of the fact that violence often brings about momentary results. Nations have frequently won their independence in battle. But, in spite of temporary victories, violence never brings permanent peace."

— A line from Dr. King's Nobel Peace Prize lecture in 1964 describing his view of violent protest

Martin Luther King, Jr. Timeline

1929 January 15   Martin is born

1944 September 20   Enters Morehouse College at age 15

1948 February 25   Ordained as Baptist preacher

1948 June 8   Graduates Morehouse College

1948 September 14   Attends Crozer Seminary

1951 May 6   Graduates Crozer Seminary

1951 September 13   Attends Boston University for Ph.D.

1953 June 18   Marries Coretta Scott

1954 September 1   Becomes pastor of Dexter Avenue Baptist Church

1955 June 5   Awarded Ph.D. and becomes Dr. Martin Luther King, Jr.

1955 November 17   Yolanda King is born

1957 January 10   Helps form the Southern Christian Leadership Conference

1957 February 18   Appears on cover of *Time* magazine

1957 October 23   Martin Luther King III is born

1960 October 19   Martin is arrested during sit-in

1961 January 31   Dexter King is born

1963 March 28   Bernice King is born

1963 March 16   Writes "Letter from Birmingham Jail"

1963 August 28   Delivers "I Have a Dream" speech on the steps of the Lincoln Memorial

World Timeline

1929   The Great Depression starts

1945 September 2   WWII ends

1948 January 30   Gandhi assassinated

1954   Vietnam War begins

1954 May 17   Brown vs. the Board of Education ruling declares "separate but equal" is not constitutional

1955 December 1   Rosa Parks is arrested for refusing to give up her seat on a public bus

1956 November 13   Browder vs Gayle ruling declares bus segregation unconstitutional

1956 December 21   Bus boycott ends and busses are integrated

1957 September 2   Nine African American students attend a previously all-white school in Little Rock, Arkansas, causing riots

1959   Alaska and Hawai'i become states

1960 February 1   The first sit-in happens in Greensboro, North Carolina

1960 November 8   John F. Kennedy elected president

1961 May 21   Freedom Riders ride integrated busses throughout the South and are attacked in Alabama

1963 May 7   Eugene "Bull" Connor approves use of powerful fire hoses, police dogs, clubs, and cattle prods on protestors in Birmingham, Alabama

1963 August 28   March on Washington draws more than 200,000 people and is televised

1963 August 30   President Kennedy is assassinated

1964 January 3   *Time* names Martin the Man of the Year

1964 March 26   Martin meets Malcolm X for the first and only time

1964 June   Martin's book *Why We Can't Wait* is published

1964 December 10   Wins Nobel Peace Prize

1965 March   Organizes Voting Rights March in Selma, Alabama

1967 June   Martin's book *Where Do We Go From Here* is published

1967 December 4   Organizes March on Poverty

1968 April 4   Martin is assassinated in Memphis, Tennessee

1983 November 2   Martin Luther King, Jr. Day becomes a national holiday

2011 August 22   Dr. Martin Luther King, Jr. monument erected in Washington, D.C.

1963 September 15   Sixteenth Street Baptist Church is bombed, killing four young black girls

1963 November 24   Lee Harvey Oswald, the man who killed President Kennedy, is shot

1965 February 21   Malcolm X is assassinated

1965 July 28   President Johnson announces more troops will be sent to Vietnam

1965 August 10   Voting Rights Act prevented voter tests and poll taxes that prevented African Americans from voting

1965 August 11   Watts riots break out in Los Angeles over police racism; they continue for five days

1967 October 2   Thurgood Marshall becomes the first African American Supreme Court Justice

1968 March 28   Chicago sanitization workers go on strike for better pay and work place safety

1968 June 5   Robert F. Kennedy is assassinated

Glossary

Abolitionist A person who wants to end slavery

Bail Money paid to a court to temporarily release a prisoner

Black Panthers A group of African Americans that defended minorities against the United States government using violence

Booker T. Washington An early supporter of civil rights who helped strengthen the economy of black communities and spoke out against racism in the early 1900s

Boycott Means refusing to support. In Montgomery, Alabama people boycotted the buses and refused to ride them, and later people boycotted lunch counters and businesses that practiced discrimination.

Brown vs. Board of Education A court case that went all the way to the Supreme Court (May 17, 1954) that essentially declared that all schools in the South must integrate.

Carpool Sharing rides to save money or time

Civil Rights The ideal of America that every American has the same rights and privileges regardless of race or background or economic status

Discrimination The practice or attitude of prejudice based on race, sex, age, nationality or some other factor

Freedom Riders Civil Rights supporters that rode buses from the North through the South to protest segregation

Henry David Thoreau Wrote *Civil Disobedience* in 1849 about protesting nonviolently against unjust laws

Integration   The opposite of "segregation" where people of all races can work, play, learn, or talk to each other without laws that oppose it

Jim Crow   Old laws, mostly-unwritten, that kept white and black people segregated in the South

John F. Kennedy   Elected President in 1960, but assassinated in 1963 in Dallas, Texas

Lyndon B. Johnson   President who followed John F. Kennedy and signed the Civil Rights Act and the Voting Rights Act into law

Malcolm X   A Civil Rights leader who disagreed with Dr. King's nonviolent approach to changing America and was later assassinated in 1965

Mohandas Gandhi   A leader of the Indian revolution against Great Britain who used non-violent forms of protest

Nobel Peace Prize   A prize established by Alfred Nobel in 1896, to honor and reward a person who has done the most for peace in the world

Nonviolent Resistance   Martin Luther King, Jr.'s approach, based on Gandhi's example in India, to changing laws that discriminated

Rosa Parks   Refused to give up her seat on the bus, starting the bus boycott movement in Montgomery, Alabama

Segregation   Where people of different races are not allowed to live, work, learn or talk with each other because it is against the law

Seminary   A school for the training of ministers to serve the church

Sit-ins   A peaceful movement staged by whites and blacks by sitting together at segregated lunch counters

Troops   A group of soldiers

Uncle Tom   A character in Harriet Beech Stowe's novel *Uncle Tom's Cabin*, the name was used negatively in the black community to say someone was too eager to win white approval

Watts   A neighborhood in South Los Angeles, California that was the source of the Watts riots

Bibliography

Adler, David. *A Picture Book of Martin Luther King, Jr.* New York: Holiday House, 1989.

King, Martin Luther, Jr., edited by Clayborne Carson. *The Autobiography of Martin Luther King, Jr.* New York: Warner Books, 1998.

Peck, Ira. *The Life and Words of Martin Luther King, Jr.* New York: Scholastic, Inc., 1991.

Rappaport, Doreen. *Martin's Big Words: The Life of Dr. Martin Luther King, Jr.* New York: Hyperion, 2001.

Siebold, Thomas, ed. *Martin Luther King, Jr.* San Diego: Greenhaven Press, Inc. 2000.

Winget, Mary. *Martin Luther King, Jr.* Minneapolis: Lerner Publications Company, 2003.

Further Reading

Bader, Bonnie. *Who Was Martin Luther King, Jr.?* New York: Grosset & Dunlap, 2007.

Farris, Christine King. *My Brother Martin: A Sister Remembers Growing Up with the Rev. Dr. Martin Luther King Jr.* New York: Aladdin, 2006.

Pastan, Amy & Primo Levi. *DK Biography: Martin Luther King, Jr.* New York: DK Children, 2004.

Norwich, Grace. *I Am Martin Luther King, Jr.* New York: Scholastic, Inc., 2012.

Index

K